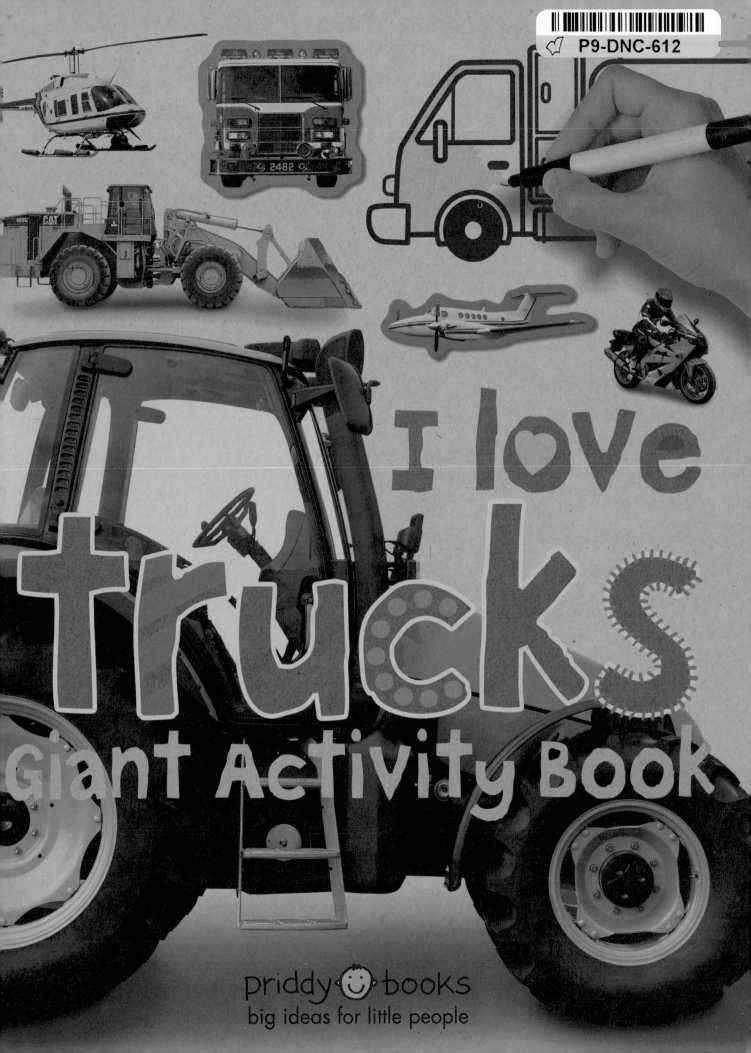

I love trucks

Giant Activity Book

priddy books
big ideas for little people

Pickup truck

It's **strong** enough for any job, however **tough**

Container truck

Carrying **heavy** goods and **LOADS** along the busy streets and roads

Tough trucks

The **snow plow** works night and **day** so the cars can drive on the roads **okay**

This **fuel tanker's** destination is the **24-hour** gas station

cable repair truck

Telephone cables fallen down? Call the repair truck into **town**

Car transporter is transporting brand new cars from night 'til morning

Counting trucks

Count the trucks and write
the totals in the boxes.

How many
backhoe
loaders can
you count?

1

How many
big rigs
can you
count?

2

How many fire trucks can you count?

How many tractors can you count?

How many dump trucks can you count? 3

How many pickup trucks can you count? 4

Amazing machines

Impress your friends with facts about these amazing machines!

5

Dump truck

These trucks have huge wheels, and can carry up to 200 tons of rocks and dirt. Can you fill in the missing letters to spell its name?

du__ t_u_k

6

Giant excavator

These machines have giant caterpillar tracks, which are as tall as a man! Can you fill in the missing letters to spell its name?

g_a_t
ex_a___t_r

Which truck can carry a huge amount of rocks and dirt?

Dot to dot

Can you connect the dots to draw the giant excavator? Then why not color in the scene?

Which truck has giant caterpillar tracks?

Bulldozer

Before the road can be **made**, it pushes and level with its **blade**

Construction

Roller

The driver sits at the **controls** as the machine spreads and **rolls**

Skid steer

Forwards, backwards, left and **right**, lifting, shifting, day and **night**

With a scratching,
scraping, grinding sound
the **scraper** scrapes
and levels the ground

Using all its
lifting power, the
crane
lifts loads up
the tower

Back bucket small,
front bucket big,
backhoe loader,
dig, dig, dig!

Big machines

Can you color in these big machines and trace over their names?

7   8   9

backhoe loader

big rig

Learn to draw

Look at the picture and the word, then trace over the outlines.

bulldozer

bulldozer

Now draw the bulldozer and fill in the letters to write its name.

b _ _ _ _ _ _ _ _

Writing practice

Trace over the outlines to write the names of the vehicles and machines.

scraper

dump truck

bus

tractor

Matching colors

Can you circle the pair of red trucks and the pair of yellow trucks?

Busy forklift truck

Can you color in this busy forklift scene?

19   20   21

Matching letters

Draw a line between each truck and the letter that its name begins with.

22

a   f

23

p   24

25

t   d

b

Mixer maze

Can you find a way through the maze to lead the construction worker to the cement mixer?

26

Start

Finish

27

Mixing and digging

Can you color in the machines and trace over their names?

28	29	30

cement mixer

31

32

33

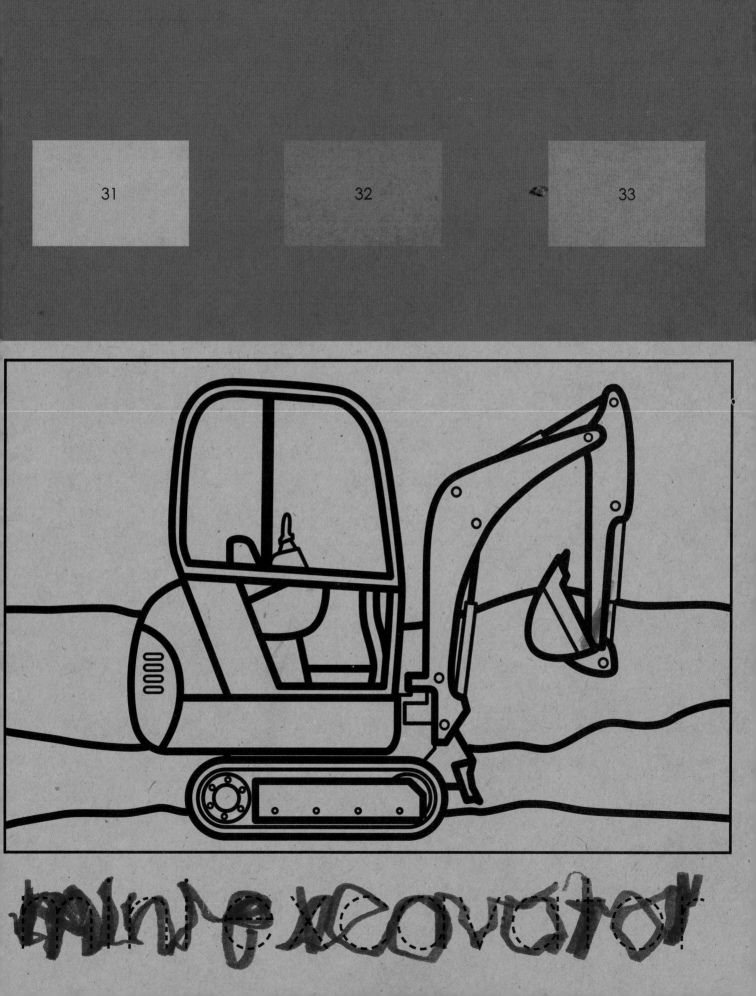

mini excavator

Dump truck carries dirt and rock night and day around the clock

Busy machines

Cement mixer
Turning, turning, round and **round**, mixing concrete for the **ground**

Digging an **enormous** crater, is the even bigger **excavator**

Moving dirt from place to place
pay loader wins the
lifting race!

The **forklift truck**
zips around, moving stuff
up and **down**

Dumper

Driving along,
bumpety bump,
carrying piles of
dirt to **dump**

What's different?

Can you spot six differences between these two pictures? Circle them on picture B.

Roller

Can you color in the roller as it spreads and rolls
the concrete? Then trace over its name.

34

35

36

roller

Learn to draw

Look at the picture and the word, then trace over the outlines.

fire truck

fire truck

Now draw the fire truck and fill in the letters to write its name.

37

f _ _ _ _   _ _ _ _ _

Missing halves

Can you draw the other halves of the pictures? Use the stickers to help you.

38

39

With so many things on the farm to **shift**, **front loader** has the **POWER** to **lift!**

John Deere 731

Combine harvester

At harvest time it rarely **stops** cutting and collecting **crops**

On the

Tractor and plow

Plow the field for seeds to sow, plant them in and watch them grow

Tracked tractor's speed is very slow, in muddy fields it's the way to go

Tractor and baler

Squish and squash hay into bales, before the rain and winter gales

farm

The farmer keeps his **tractor** clean because it is his best **machine**

Plowing the field

Can you color in this busy plowing scene?

40	41	42

How many birds can you count?

Letter practice

Trace over the outlines to practice writing letters.

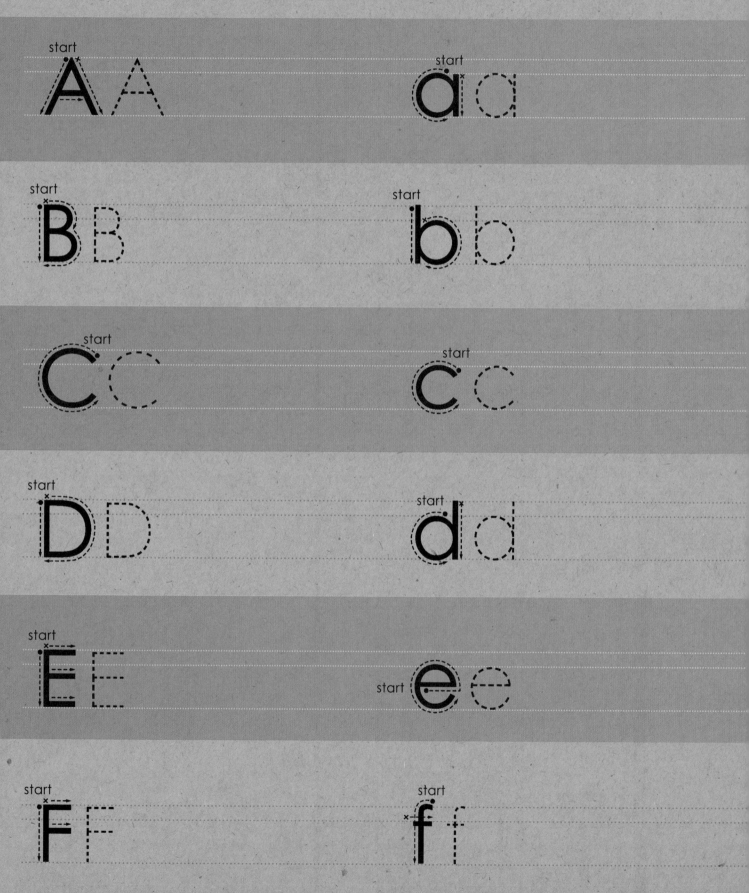

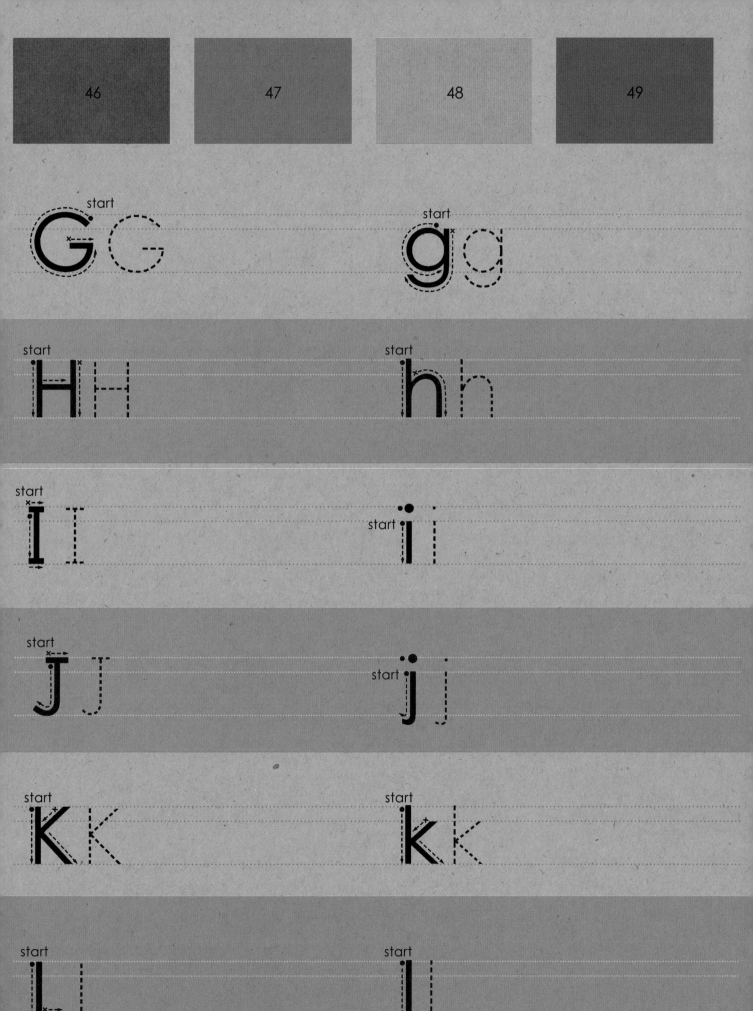

46

47

48

49

start
G G

start
g g

start
H H

start
h h

start
I I

start
i i

start
J J

start
j j

start
K K

start
k k

start
L L

start
l l

Letter practice

Trace over the outlines to practice writing letters.

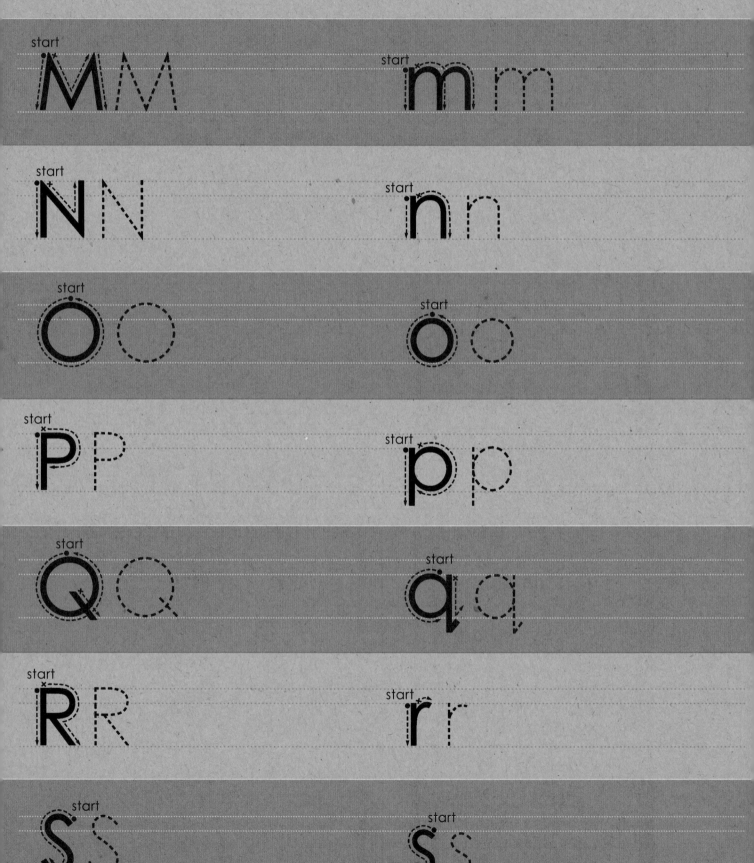

start M M M

start m m m

start N N N

start n n n

start O O O

start o o o

start P P P

start p p p

start Q Q Q

start q q q

start R R R

start r r r

start S S S

start s s s

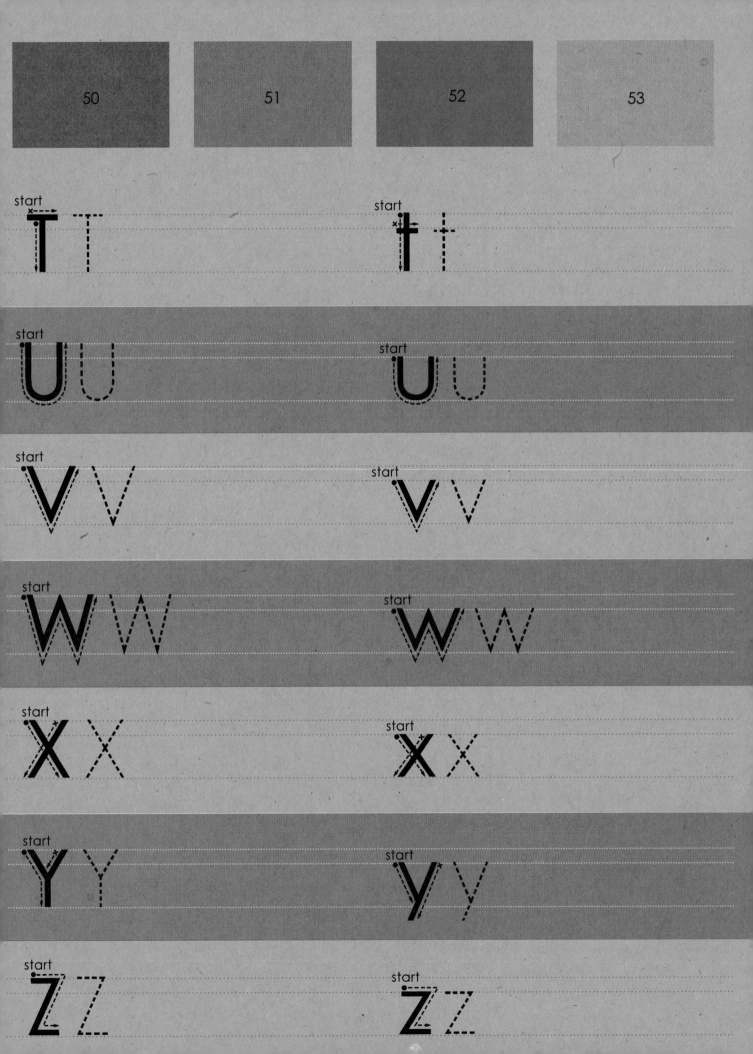

Drag bike
waiting on the tarmac **strip,**
throttle up and **let it rip!**

speeds and skids
down forest **tracks,**
rally car racing to the **max**

Motor sports

The Grand Prix car is in first **place,**
about to win a fantastic **race**

Monster truck

With awesome power
and **wheels so fat,**
it crushes cars until
they're **flat!**

As it races down
the straight the
stock car
will accelerate

Racing around the
turns and **bumps,**
dirt bike roars,
skids and **jumps**

On the road

Can you color in these vehicles and trace over their names?

54   55   56

sports car

57

58

59

scooter

Learn to draw

Look at the picture and the word, then trace over the outlines.

dump truck | dump truck

Now draw the dump truck and fill in the letters to write its name.

60

d___ _____

Adding trucks

Write the number of trucks in the boxes, then add them up.

61 $+$  $=$

☐ ☐ ☐

62 $+$ 63 $=$

☐ ☐ ☐

64 $+$ $=$

☐ ☐ ☐

Coloring time

Color in the pictures, using the stickers to help you.

construction worker

65

skid steer

66

big rig

67

mini excavator

68

Missing letters

Can you fill in the missing letters to complete
the machine and vehicle names?

g_ide_

69

_ra_n

v_n

70

b_ll_o_er

Car transporter

Can you color in the busy car transporter? Then trace over its name.

71   72   73

car transporter

Snow plow

Color in the snow plow, then trace over its name.

74   75   76

snow plow

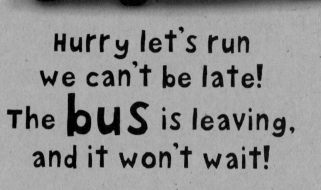

Taking my **Mini** for a spin, leaves me with a great big grin!

Hurry let's run we can't be late! The **bus** is leaving, and it won't wait!

On the road

City car Zipping around the city **streets**, it beeps its horn to all it **meets**

Huge wheels and tires, high above the ground. This big yellow **Hummer** is the toughest truck around

Shiny silver, bright and clean,
the **sports car** is
a speed machine!

Minivan
There are lots of seats
for you and me,
on a **road trip**
with the family

Motorcycle
I really love the
way it **feels**
to race around
on just two
wheels

Motorcycle Scene

Can you decorate the motorcycle scene?
Look at the pictures below for ideas, add the
ones you like to the scene, then color it in!

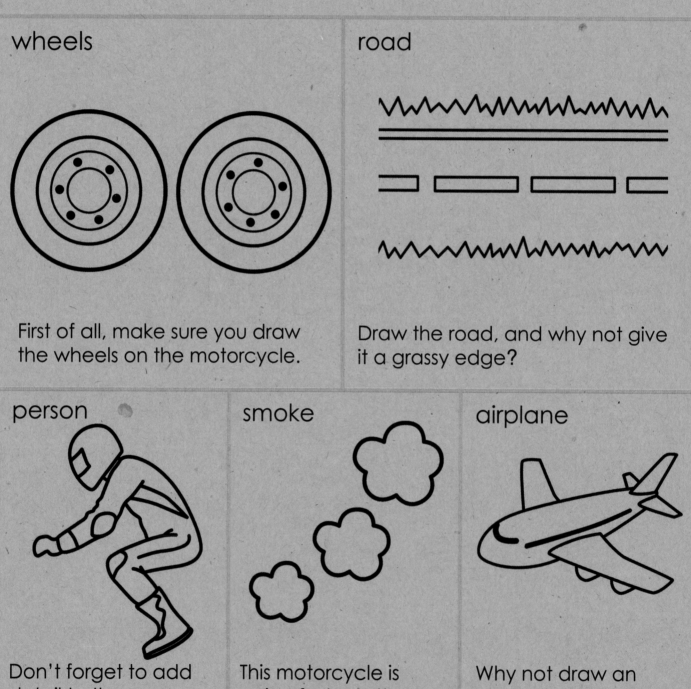

wheels

First of all, make sure you draw
the wheels on the motorcycle.

road

Draw the road, and why not give
it a grassy edge?

person

Don't forget to add
detail to the person
riding the motorcycle!

smoke

This motorcycle is
going fast, so draw
some smoke behind it!

airplane

Why not draw an
airplane flying high
above in the sky?

Follow the lines

Can you trace over the lines to lead the workers to their trucks?

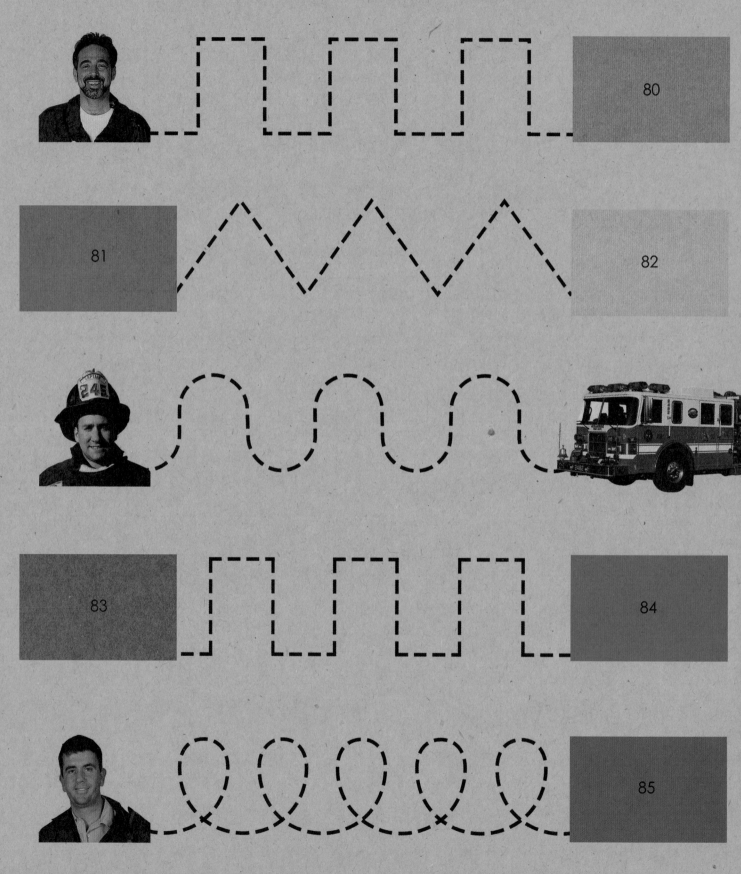

All-terrain vehicle

Can you color in the speedy all-terrain vehicle?

86.   87   88

Amazing Vehicles

Impress your friends with facts about these amazing vehicles!

91

92

89

Racecar

Racecars are very light, but hugely powerful. They can reach super speeds of 230 mph.

90

Superbike

Superbikes can reach speeds of 195 mph. When cornering, the driver leans so the bike doesn't fall over.

4x4 truck

4x4 trucks have very large wheels, and super powerful engines.

All-terrain vehicle

All-terrain vehicles have strong suspensions, so they can travel over all terrains.

Which vehicle do you have to ride carefully when cornering?

Word search

Can you find the five words in the word search?

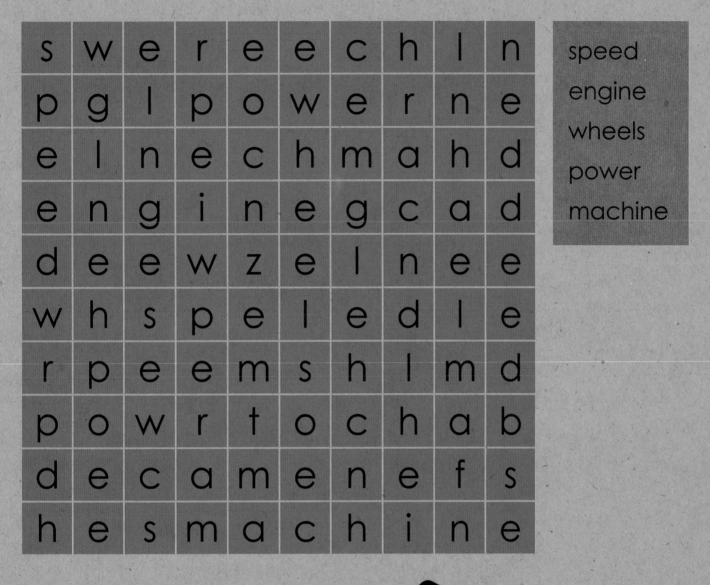

s	w	e	r	e	e	c	h	l	n
p	g	l	p	o	w	e	r	n	e
e	l	n	e	c	h	m	a	h	d
e	n	g	i	n	e	g	c	a	d
d	e	e	w	z	e	l	n	e	e
w	h	s	p	e	l	e	d	l	e
r	p	e	e	m	s	h	l	m	d
p	o	w	r	t	o	c	h	a	b
d	e	c	a	m	e	n	e	f	s
h	e	s	m	a	c	h	i	n	e

speed

engine

wheels

power

machine

Which is your favorite of these vehicles?

Monorail

rides around the **park**,
all day long from
dawn 'til **dark**

Mountain train

Here comes the train,
clickety clack,
to the top
of the mountain and **back**

On the tracks

Subway train

Underground from station
to **station** - it's the city's
fastest **transportation**

Snow plow

clearing a way through the
snow, then along the
track the train can go

Freight train

Loaded up with tons of **freight**, city to coast and never **late**

Eurostar

I think I got the briefest **glance** of a high-speed train that's off to **FRANCE**

You catch a **streetcar** on the street. Step aboard and find a seat

When in JAPAN don't go by plane, just take the speedy **bullet train**

Speedy trains

Can you color in the trains and trace over their names?

93	94	95

bullet train

monorail

Adding trucks

Write the number of trucks in the boxes, then add them up.

99 $+$ 100 $=$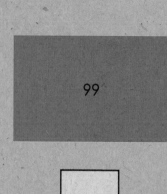

[ ] [ ] [ ]

101 $+$ 102 $=$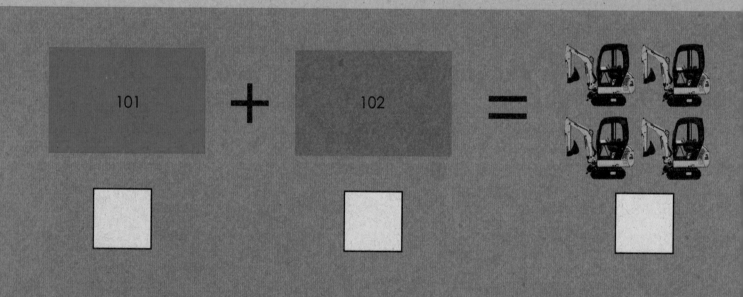

[ ] [ ] [ ]

103 $+$ 104 $=$

[ ] [ ] [ ]

Word search

Can you find the machines and vehicles in the word search?

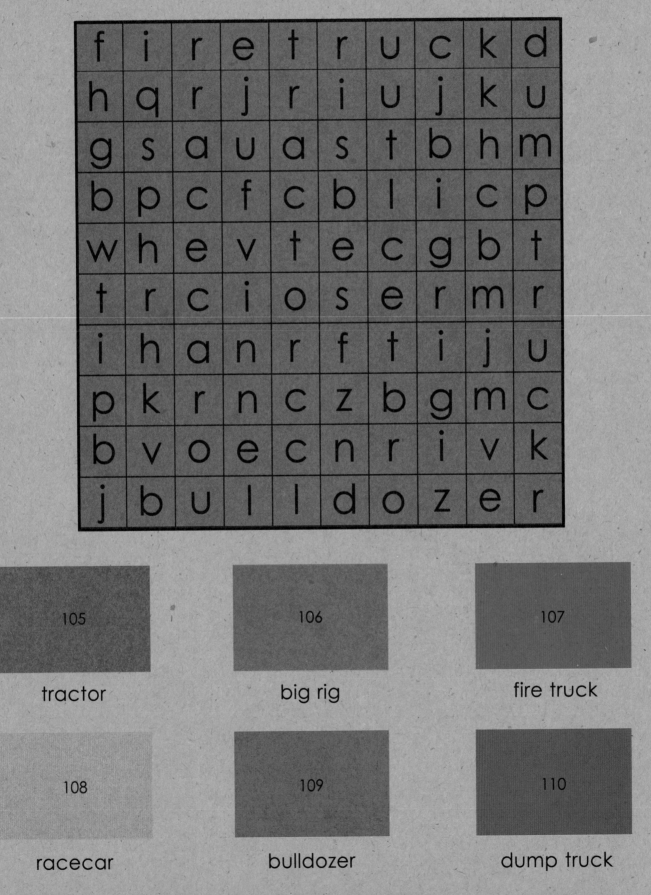

f	i	r	e	t	r	u	c	k	d
h	q	r	j	r	i	u	j	k	u
g	s	a	u	a	s	t	b	h	m
b	p	c	f	c	b	l	i	c	p
w	h	e	v	t	e	c	g	b	t
t	r	c	i	o	s	e	r	m	r
i	h	a	n	r	f	t	i	j	u
p	k	r	n	c	z	b	g	m	c
b	v	o	e	c	n	r	i	v	k
j	b	u	l	l	d	o	z	e	r

105

tractor

106

big rig

107

fire truck

108

racecar

109

bulldozer

110

dump truck

Passenger jet

We're in the air and on our way
to our summer holiday

In the air

Red Arrow roars
and thrills the crowds,
streaming smoke trails
through the clouds

Glider
silent swooping through
the sky, soaring,
drifting way up high

Hot air balloons

The burning flames
make them lift
into the sky
and then they drift

Helicopter

Space Shuttle

Roaring, burning
rocket blast, zoom up
to space super fast

Hovering high above the
ground, rotor blades spin
round and round

Hot air balloons

Can you color in the hot air balloons to make this scene look really great?

111

112

113

Which hot air balloon is your favorite?

Rocket maze

Can you find a way through the maze to lead the rocket back to Earth?

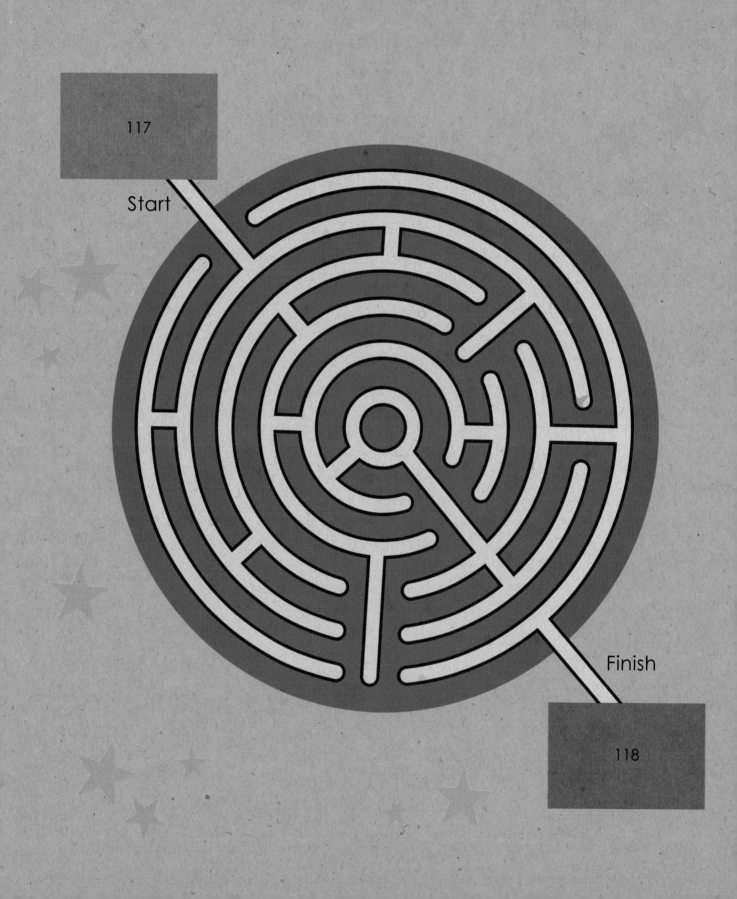

117

Start

Finish

118

Writing practice

Trace over the outlines to write the words below.

firefighter

motorcycle

fuel tanker

helicopter

Glider

Color in the glider and trace over its name.

| 119 | 120 | 121 |

glider

School bus

Do you travel to school on a bus? Color in the bus, then trace over its name.

| 122 | 123 | 124 |

school bus

What's different?

Can you spot six differences between these two pictures? Circle them on picture B.

125

A

B

Learn to draw

Look at the picture and the word, then trace over the outlines.

delivery truck

delivery truck

Now draw the delivery truck and fill in the letters to write its name.

126

d_____

t_____

Flying high

Can you color in the airplanes to make this scene really busy and bright?

| 127 | 128 | 129 |

How many airplanes can you count?

130

131

132

Amazing machines

Impress your friends with facts about these amazing machines.

133

134

135

136

Jumbo jet

These huge airplanes can carry up to 600 passengers and fly at speeds of 565 mph.

Space Shuttle

When Space Shuttles are launched, the rocket engines burn thousands of gallons of fuel every minute!

Container ship

Huge container ships transport many different types of goods all around the world.

Bullet train

Bullet trains can carry more than 1,300 passengers, and travel at speeds of 200 mph.

Which machine can carry up to 600 passengers?

Coloring time

Can you color in the airport scene?

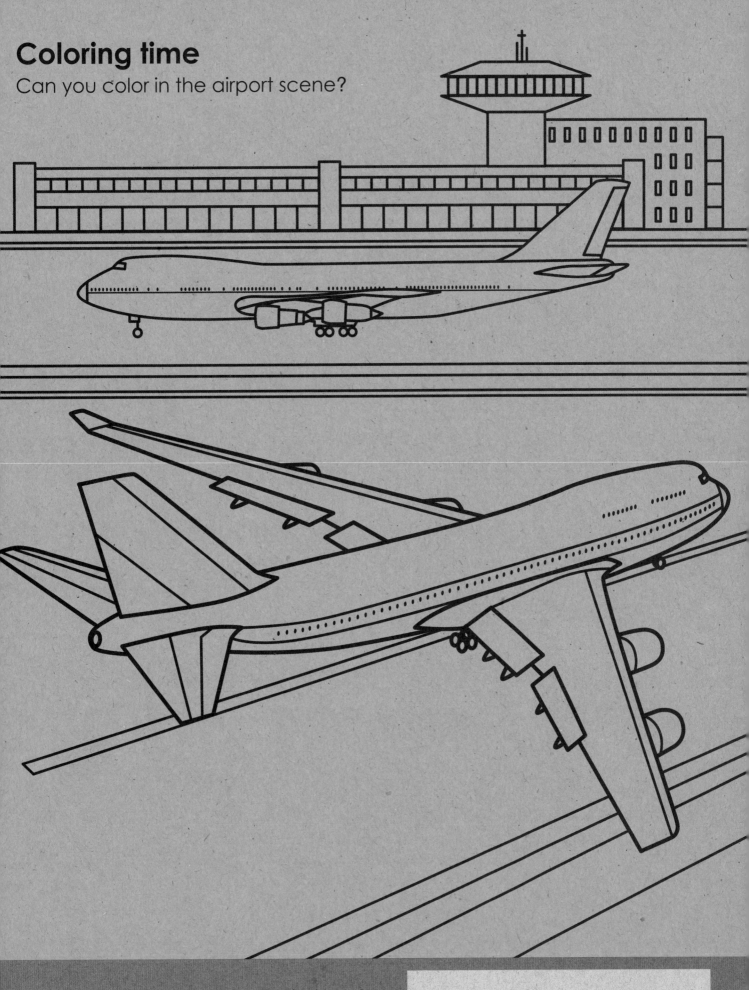

Have you ever been on an airplane?

Number practice

Trace over the outlines to practice writing numbers.

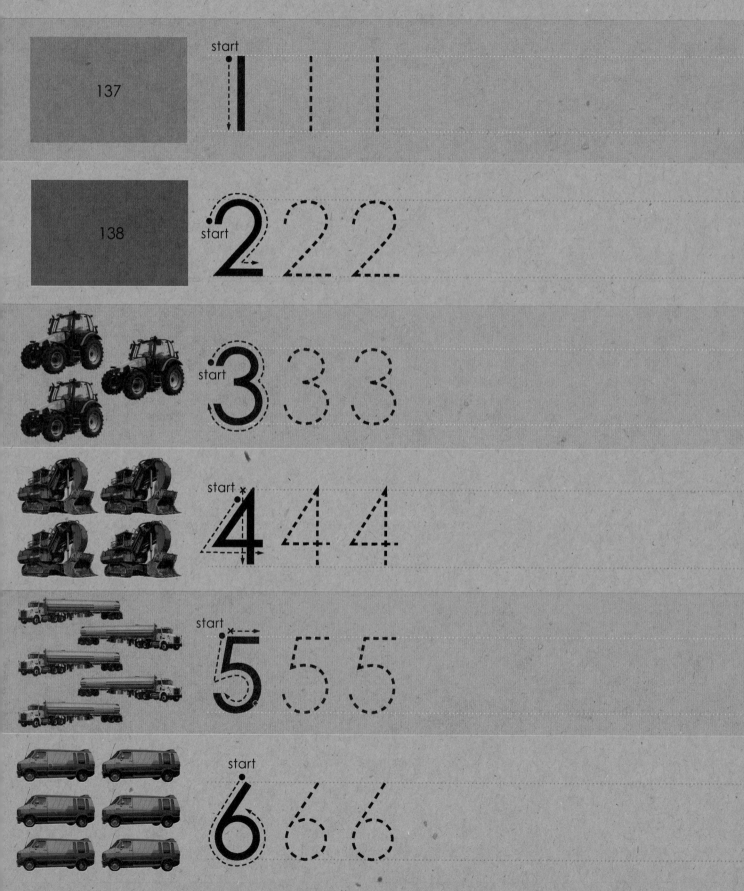

137

start
1 1 1

138

start
2 2 2

start
3 3 3

start
4 4 4

start
5 5 5

start
6 6 6

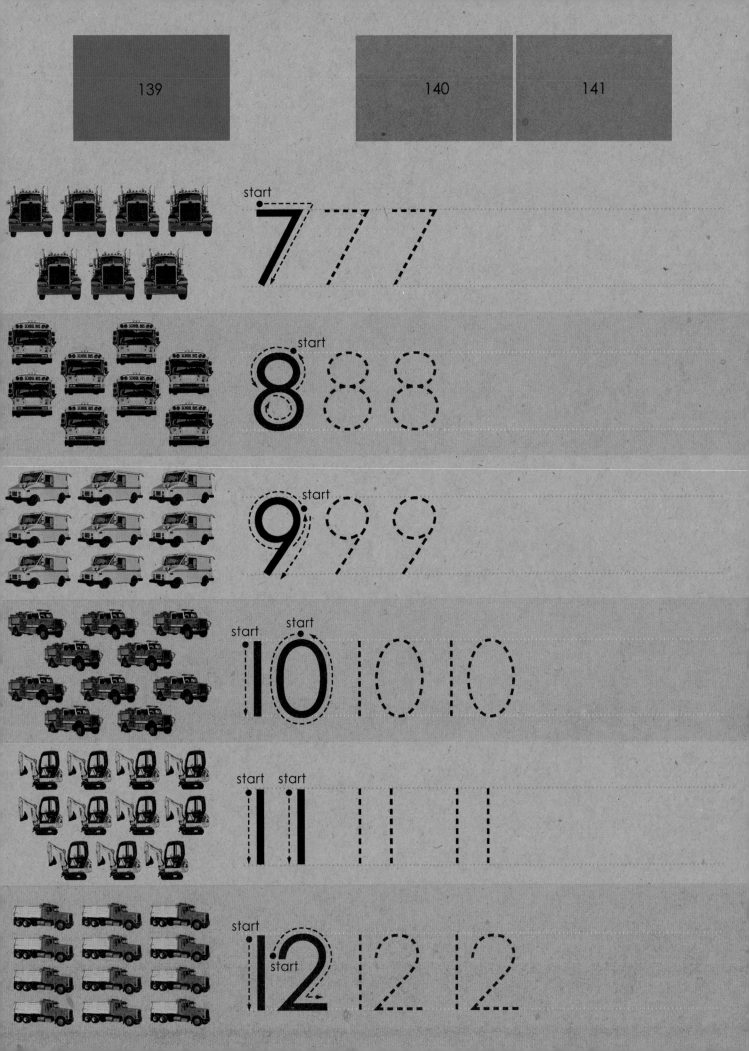

139

140

141

start
7 7 7 7

start
8 8 8

start
9 9 9

start start
10 10 10

start start
11 11 11

start
start
12 12 12

Ladder truck

Raise the ladder higher and higher
to rescue people from the fire

Rescue Vehicles

The **rescue truck** is on its way
to help the people and save the day

Ambulance
staying ready,
on **alert** to help
the people
who've been hurt

Sirens screaming,
bright lights flashing,
city streets,
police car
dashing

Airport fire truck

Sat by the runway just in **case**
to a fire it has to **race**

Odd one out

Which picture is different from all the others?

firefighter

fire chief's truck

fire truck

helicopter pilot

Emergency maze

Can you find a way through the maze to lead the paramedic to the ambulance?

142

Start

Finish

143

Linking lines

Can you draw a line between each truck and the color it matches?

blue

yellow

144

orange

145

red

146

green

white

Sticker search

Can you find the fire truck stickers?

147

148

149

150

151

152

Police trail

Which trail will lead the police officer to her car?

How many?

Count the trucks and write the number of each in the boxes.

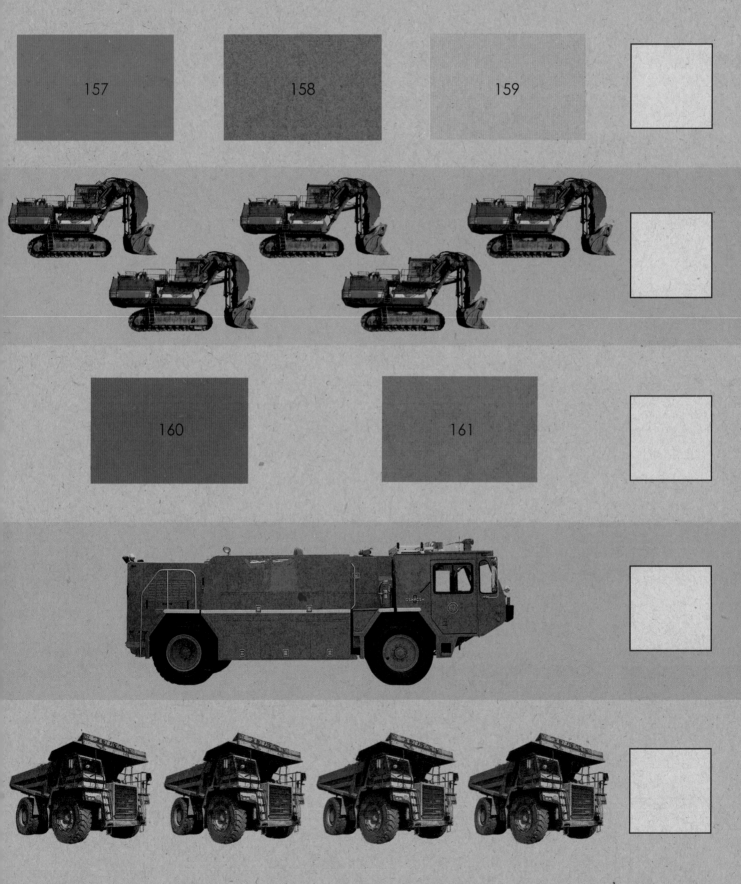

157

158

159

160

161

Counting trucks

Count the trucks and write the totals in the boxes.

How many
red trucks
can you
count?

162

How many
blue trucks
can you
count?

163

How many white
trucks can
you count?

How many yellow
trucks can
you count?

How many
green trucks
can you
count?

164

How many
black trucks
can you
count?

165

On the construction site

Can you color in this busy scene to make it look really great?

Exactly the same

Only two fire trucks are exactly the same. Can you circle them?

A

B

C

D

E

F

Mix and match

Can you draw lines between the pairs of matching trucks?

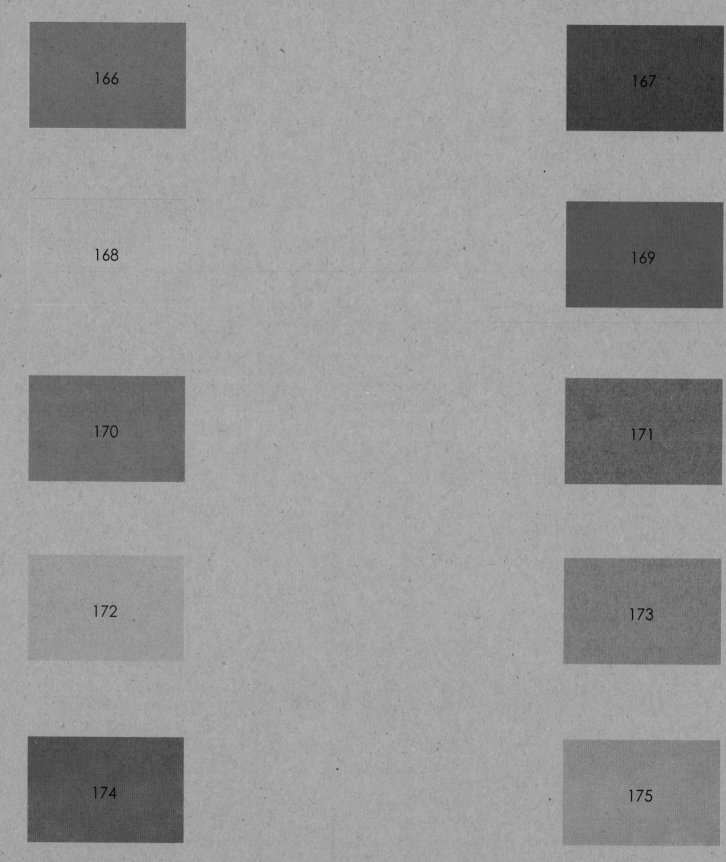

Dot to dot

Connect the dots to draw the picture of the big rig, then color it in using the colored dots as a guide.

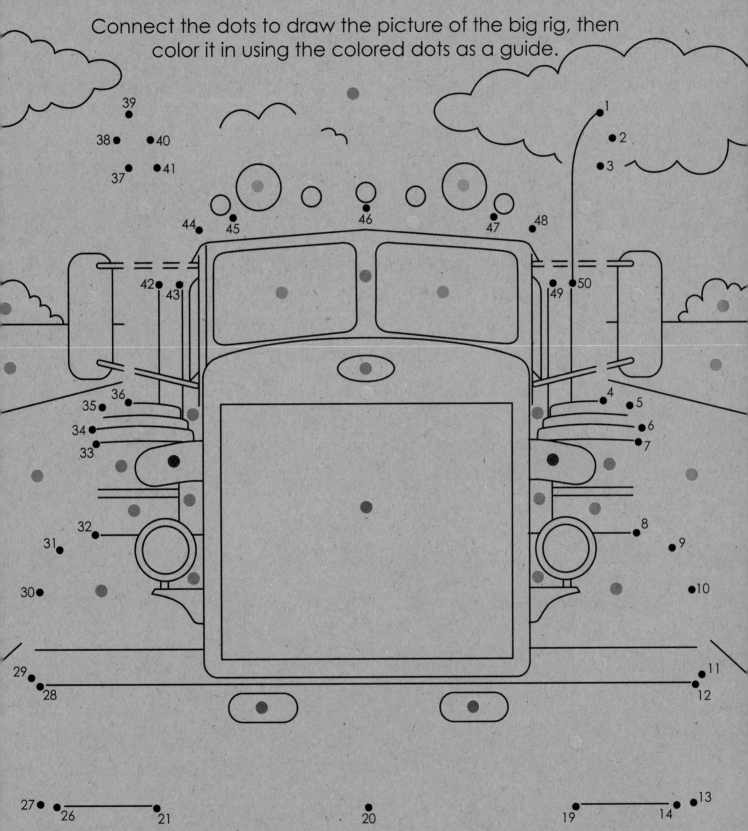

Carrying goods from far away,
the **container ship** sails all day

On the water

Passenger boat

Tugboat

Working hard around the clock, helping ships into the dock

All aboard
we're off today
for a **pleasant** trip around the bay

Sailboat

Push off the quay and hoist the sail, let's go before it blows a gale!

Cruise ship

There is lots to do and lots to see, come **cruising** on the ship with me

Speedboat

Step on board and pay the fare, the **water taxi** takes us there

Hold on **TIGHT** you must be brave, the speedboat jumps from **wave to wave**

Busy boats

Can you color in the busy boats and trace over their names?

176   177   178

fishing boat

179

180

181

motor yacht

Amazing boats

Impress your friends with facts about these amazing boats!

182

183

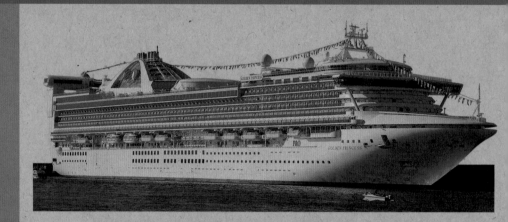

Cruise ship
These huge ships take people around the world. Some are so big that they have swimming pools and tennis courts on board! Have you ever seen a cruise ship?

yes

no

Speedboat
Speedboats can reach speeds of 80 mph, and the boat lifts up at the front when going really fast. What color is the speedboat?

red

yellow

green

Which ship can have swimming pools and tennis courts on board?

How many?

Can you count how many police boats, cruise ships, ferries and sailboats there are? Write the answers in the boxes.

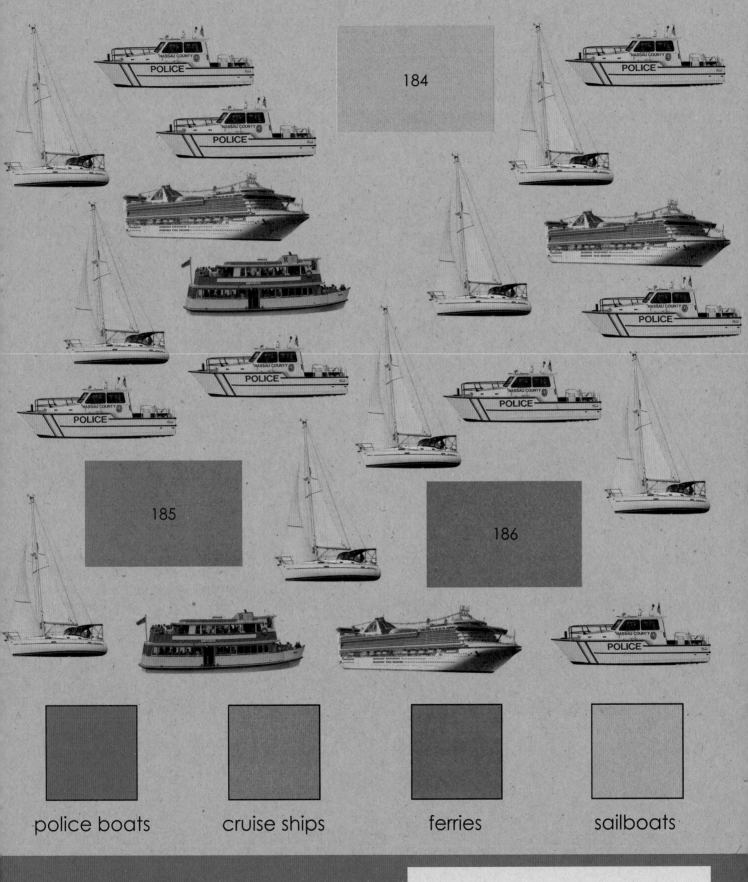

184

185

186

police boats

cruise ships

ferries

sailboats

Which is your favorite boat?

Mix and match

Can you draw lines between the pairs of matching vehicles?

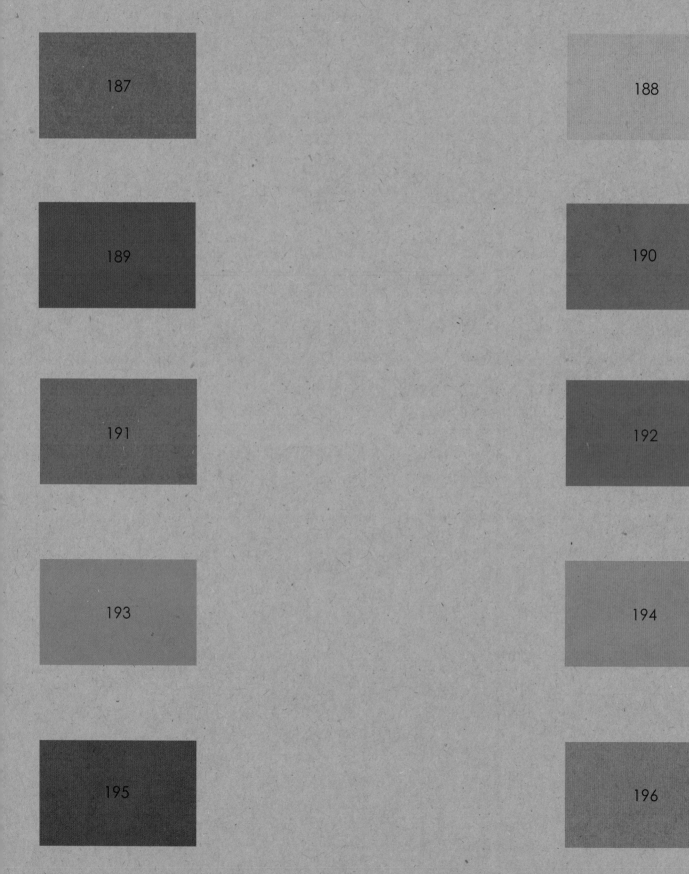

How many?

Count the vehicles and write the totals in the boxes.

Dot to dots

Connect the dots to draw the pictures, then color them in using the colored dots as a guide.

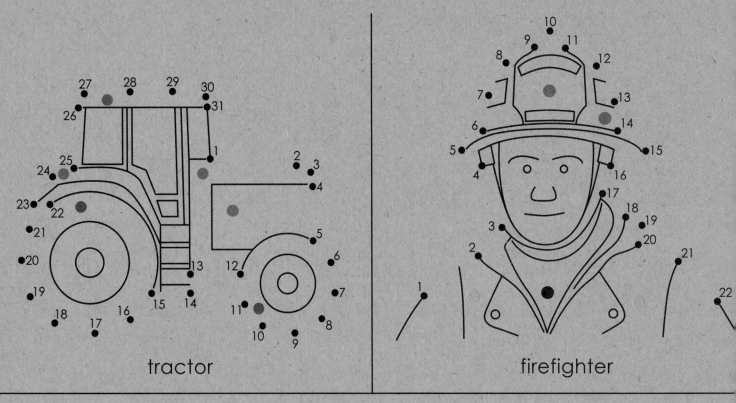

tractor

firefighter

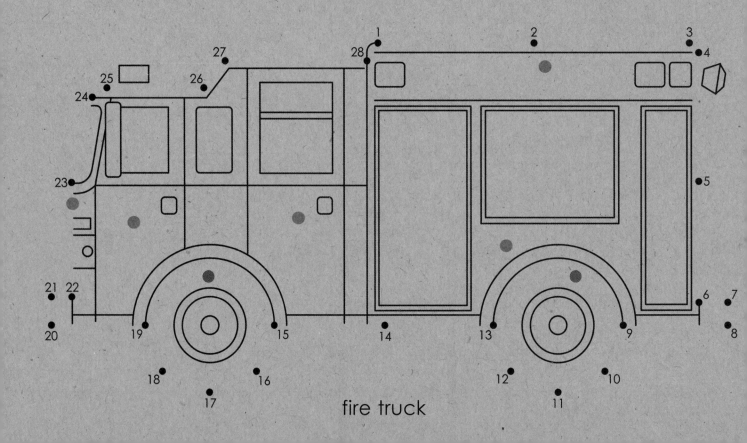

fire truck